CELEBRATING THE FAMILY NAME OF DEVI

Celebrating the Family Name of Devi

Walter the Educator

Silent King Books
a WhichHead Entertainment Imprint

Copyright © 2024 by Walter the Educator

All rights reserved. No part of this book may be reproduced in any manner whatsoever without written permission except in the case of brief quotations embodied in critical articles and reviews.

First Printing, 2024

Disclaimer

This book is a literary work; the story is not about specific persons, locations, situations, and/or circumstances unless mentioned in a historical context. Any resemblance to real persons, locations, situations, and/or circumstances is coincidental. This book is for entertainment and informational purposes only. The author and publisher offer this information without warranties expressed or implied. No matter the grounds, neither the author nor the publisher will be accountable for any losses, injuries, or other damages caused by the reader's use of this book. The use of this book acknowledges an understanding and acceptance of this disclaimer.

Celebrating the Family Name of Devi is a memory book that belongs to the Celebrating Family Name Book Series by Walter the Educator. Collect them all and more books at WaltertheEducator.com

USE THE EXTRA SPACE TO DOCUMENT YOUR FAMILY MEMORIES THROUGHOUT THE YEARS

DEVI

Beneath the sun's eternal glow,

The name of Devi starts to grow.

A name of grace, both fierce and kind,

A legacy of heart and mind.

Born of earth and kissed by skies,

The name of Devi never dies.

It weaves through time, both near and far,

A guiding light, a shining star.

From verdant fields to palace halls,

The Devi name resounds, it calls.

With wisdom vast and spirits high,

They rise as mountains touch the sky.

A lineage steeped in sacred lore,

A strength that flows from every shore.

The Devi name, a timeless song,

A rhythm steady, proud, and strong.

In every step, in every breath,

They face the world, defying death.

A family born of endless might,

Through darkest storms, they find the light.

Through vibrant art and melodies,

The Devi name sways with the breeze.

A legacy of love and care,

A bond unbroken, ever rare.

From scholars' pens to warriors' shields,

The Devi name its power wields.

A force of truth, a voice of peace,

Their timeless echoes never cease.

With every dawn, the name inspires,

A spark to kindle ancient fires.

In hearts it dwells, a steady flame,

The world remembers Devi's name.

Through generations, bold and free,

The Devi name shapes destiny.

A family vast, yet closely tied,

A spirit strong, a boundless pride.

So let us sing of Devi's grace,

A name that time cannot erase.

A shining thread in life's great loom,

Forever bright, forever in bloom.

ABOUT THE CREATOR

Walter the Educator is one of the pseudonyms for Walter Anderson. Formally educated in Chemistry, Business, and Education, he is an educator, an author, a diverse entrepreneur, and he is the son of a disabled war veteran. "Walter the Educator" shares his time between educating and creating. He holds interests and owns several creative projects that entertain, enlighten, enhance, and educate, hoping to inspire and motivate you. Follow, find new works, and stay up to date with Walter the Educator™ at WaltertheEducator.com

www.ingramcontent.com/pod-product-compliance
Lightning Source LLC
LaVergne TN
LVHW012051070526
838201LV00082B/3908